I LOVE THE BEACH

For Carl

I love everything at the beach:
the patterns the wind and waves
make on the sand;
the marram grass,
like hair that won't sit down;
sticks bleached white and smooth
by the rubbing of the sea's fingers;
birds, like scraps of paper
tossed high, high in the sky.

3

On cold dark days,
the sea hisses and growls—
a monster, slapping his great
wet footsteps up the sand.
The sea combs my hair
with fresh-cold fingers.
The whole world
seems clean and free and wide.

4

There are a hundred treasures
to find in the sand:
shells and seaweed;
tangled ropes
washed up from fishing boats;
sad, dead seagulls;
pieces of fishing net;
driftwood in strange shapes.

6

I always find something to take home.
Sometimes, it is a thick stalk of kelp to cut into balls
that will bounce.
Or a sea-washed bottle, its sides crusted with a whole city
of barnacle houses.
Who knows? One day I may find a message in a bottle.

Among the rugged rocks
lie small sea-worlds.
Tiny fish dart in and out
of swaying seaweed fronds.
Sea anemones beckon
with many fingers.
Shellfish slide along the walls,
silent creatures in a silent world.

When the sun shines,
the sea becomes an endless mass
of blue, blue ripples,
edged with creaming foam.
It whispers cool songs.
The dry sand feels like warm silk
under my bare feet.

When I run,
the dry sand spurts out
behind my feet
in sudden little sprays.

I trickle it through
parted fingers,
and, like water running,
it pours between them,
smooth and flowing.

15

I climb to the top
of a sandhill mountain
and shout loudly
under the blue bowl
of the sky,
"I am King!"

The grasses bow at my feet,
while the seagulls screech and wheel.
And I jump
down to the bottom of the sandhill,
showering sand like rain.

When I grow up,
I could be a sailor on a ship
that goes far out across the ocean,
until our beach,
and then our country,
are just fading specks.

In days of old,
I could have been a pirate!
"Heave ho, me hearties!"
I'd wave my cutlass at my fearsome crew.
And those who didn't obey
would have to walk the plank.

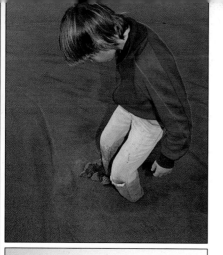

Where the tide has marked
the sand with wetness,
I stand and trample my feet
up and down, up and down.
The sand turns to porridge,
clinging around my ankles.
Then, in comes the cold rush
of waves on my shins.

Beyond the reach of the tide, where the sand lies firm, but damp, I use a sea-tossed stick to write important messages.

I like the beach best when there aren't many people there.
The sea and sand and sky all belong to me.